MY AUTISM JOURNAL

T0282791

First published in Great Britain in 2024 by Jessica Kingsley Publishers
An imprint of John Murray Press

1

Copyright © Carly Jones 2024
Illustrations Copyright © Nicky Borowiec 2024

Front cover image illustration © Nicky Borowiec 2024.

A CIP catalogue record for this title is available from the British Library and the Library of Congress

ISBN 978 1 83997 434 2

Printed and bound in Great Britain by Bell & Bain Limited

Jessica Kingsley Publishers' policy is to use papers that are natural, renewable and recyclable products and made from wood grown in sustainable forests. The logging and manufacturing processes are expected to conform to the environmental regulations of the country of origin.

Jessica Kingsley Publishers
Carmelite House
50 Victoria Embankment
London EC4Y 0DZ

www.jkp.com

John Murray Press
Part of Hodder & Stoughton Ltd
An Hachette Company

MY AUTISM JOURNAL

CONCEPT BY CARLY JONES, CONTENT BY <u>YOU</u>

Jessica Kingsley Publishers
London and Philadelphia

Dedicated to Jon who works tirelessly at the NHS to support people in crisis and who has made my daily entries in my journal much happier ones.

"The more safe and happy you REALLY are with someone, chances are, the less you'll have to mask or pretend to be someone you're not around them."

– CARLY X

INTRODUCTION

HELLO MY NAME IS:

CARLY JONES

ME!

HELLO!

My name is Carly. I live in Berkshire in the UK, with my daughters and a very large dog named Hunter.

I am an Autistic woman and also a mum to Autistic girls. I didn't know I was Autistic until I was 32 years old, which meant I grew up not understanding why life was so different for me.

I struggled with school, university, keeping safe, eating properly, friendships and understanding what "happens next", be that day-by-day or week-by-week.

I really wish that back then others had known that I was Autistic and that I knew it as well. Why? Because if my trusted adults had known how I was feeling and what I needed support with (and when I was ok to do something without being held back too much!),

school
     friendships
          keeping safe
               living a healthy life

would all have been much easier.

I also wish that other trusted adults had known my strengths and talents and I wish they had understood that when I became fascinated by something new, it wasn't a phase or something silly, but was something I was greatly interested in.

I wish they had known my interests could make me feel happy and less lonely, and, one day, could even become a job for me!

WHY DID WE CREATE THIS JOURNAL?

I wrote a book that came out just before Christmas 2021. It's called *Safeguarding Autistic Girls: Strategies for Professionals*. In it, I wrote down ideas for professionals who help Autistic teens keep safe and healthy.

Many doctors, parents and others commented that it would be helpful if Autistic teens had an easy way to track their own safety, happiness and health – and that's where this book steps in. It's a journal with tips and advice, as well as prompts to help you record your own thoughts and experiences.

If you wish, you can share it day-by-day or week-by-week with your trusted adults so they can help you.

Asking for help can be extremely difficult for Autistic people of all ages. To ask for help we have to jump several hurdles:

HURDLE 1 – Knowing what we are feeling or experiencing isn't healthy, helpful, or good for us.

HURDLE 2 – Knowing that our loved ones and/or trusted adult doesn't already know what we are going through and that we need to tell them for them to know.

HURDLE 3 – Knowing that other people, when they know, can help can make it stop or make it better.

LET'S TALK BOUNDARIES!

The journal looks and works much like a private diary. If you want to use it JUST FOR YOU then it should be for your eyes only.

However, the journal may have been be gifted to you in the hope that it becomes a way of sharing information with your trusted adults too. So it's best to have a chat with them to make it clear who (if anyone) has permission to read it.

It is YOUR CHOICE how you want to benefit from the journal. Have a think about it.

Do you want it just for you and NOBODY else to read?

Or do you want to share the journey with your parents, doctors, teachers or other trusted adults, so they can help keep you safe and happy, and find out how to best support you?

Neither choice is wrong, there is no right or wrong way to use the journal. What is important is that your boundaries are respected and that information is only shared with those you want to see it, and who have your best interests at heart. You need to trust these people not to share the information somewhere unsafe or embarrassing for you.

You'll see that there's a section at the end of the journal which is for the trusted adults you choose to share everything with. You can read this too, if you want! It's there to explain the boundaries to them too, and to give them advice so they can help you in the best ways possible.

If it was 14-year-old me thinking who I would like to share my journal with, I would have chosen:

- Me!

- my parents

- my Head of Year (who was lovely)

...but ABSOLUTELY NO ONE ELSE. Definitely not all my teachers as I only trusted my Head of Year with my personal stuff. And definitely not friends. Sometimes I had friends who I would share private things with, but they would then tell everyone and it was horrible.

In fact, I'd recommend that you only share the journal with trusted adults and not friends your own age, even if you are really close to them, and even if they are also Autistic or about to be diagnosed as Autistic.

Sounds a bit mean, doesn't it? There are good reasons to not share your journal with other people your age though. Trusted safe adults have a responsibility to keep you safe while friends don't have a legal or parental responsibility to do that.

We have two types of trust in life:

- affective trust, which comes from our heart but is high risk (this is when you just feel you can trust someone),

- cognitive trust, which comes from our head and is often used by (good!) professionals (this is when we're told we can trust someone).

Sharing your journal means you'll have to find a mix of heart and head trust – who do you feel you can trust and who do you know you can trust?

Putting your daily emotions and activities down on paper and then passing those to someone else can leave you feeling vulnerable. It's not easy, so take things at your own pace. Remember you can change your mind and decide that something should remain private, just for you, at any time.

You can use this space to write down the people you want to be able to read your journal. If that's just you, that's ok too.

THE FOLLOWING PEOPLE ARE ALLOWED TO READ MY JOURNAL:

HOW TO USE THIS JOURNAL

ALL ABOUT ME

The All About Me pages are for you to introduce yourself to whoever will be reading your journal and, in a way, to introduce yourself to YOU. Seems odd, doesn't it, to think we have to introduce ourselves to ourselves but there is a good, healthy, happy reason for doing so.

Being Autistic, especially before we know about this side of our identity, we can spend a lot of our life trying our best to fit in. Sometimes we copy what other people like and what other people do to make them like or accept us or even just to get by.

You may find sometimes in a social situation, you say "yes" a lot or agree with what others say, simply to avoid standing out or to ensure there isn't a debate!

Saying "yes" and people-pleasing can be difficult as, over time, we slowly forget our own likes, wants, beliefs, ambitions and plans.

If we don't have the time to think about ourselves then it can make us very sad and mentally unhappy. Writing down our favourite things can help us remember who we really are after a day of fitting in and trying to please others. Here are some tips on what you may like to add, but remember, it is your journal so feel free to ignore my tips completely and do your own thing!

NAME

This is where you will write your name. It could be fancy, your full name, a nickname you have for yourself or even another name you like to use or go by.

Maybe you could add your real name and then the name you would have chosen for yourself? Have fun with it!

Want to be a doctor one day? Add Dr as well!

AGE

Write your age here. It could be in years or if you're far smarter than I am, feel free to do this in how many months, weeks, days, hours old you are!

Do you like planets? How old are you in Mars years?

Like animals? How old are you in dog, cat, mouse years? Who shares your birthday? A famous celebrity? A footballer? Anyone Royal? What happened on the day you were born in the news? Write it all down or simply add your age, it's your choice!

MY BIGGEST TALENTS

Ok there is only ONE rule here: I need you to promise you won't write "nothing". Leaving it blank is fine, just do not write down "NO talents". Even if we think we don't have a talent, we do. Autistic people young and not so young have something they are good at and something that makes them happy.

Being Autistic we often assume that because WE can do it, think it, create it, everyone else can too. That is false, it really is fake news! Not everyone knows everything YOU know, not everyone can create what you can, not everyone can do what you can do.

- Are you a good artist?
- Footballer?
- Writer?
- Singer?
- Swimmer?
- Pet-sitter?
- Horse-rider?
- Animation movie-watcher?
- Do you spot the mistakes in films and TV shows?
- Do you know any films, songs or poems off by heart?
- What's your memory like?
- Do you have a good long-term memory?
- Are you curious?
- Do you ever look at a penny and instead of just seeing a penny you look at the date on the penny and wonder what happened that year in history?
- Do you have an eye for detail?
- Can you research all the breeds of sharks, dinosaurs, birds?
- Are you loyal, honest, trustworthy?
- Are you always early for parties, school, college or University?
- Are you kind when others are cruel?
- Are you always the first to help people in need?
- Are you good at knowing when someone needs you or when something happened?
- Are you able to find a joke in any situation and make something sad, happy?

One of my favourite films (made from the book, *Girl, Interrupted* by Susanna Kaysen) has a line in it that says

*"I told her once I wasn't good at anything.
She told me survival is a talent."*

Do you try to be strong even when things are really tough? THAT'S a huge skill that many other people don't have, and one that will take you very far in life, even if you haven't considered it as a talent before.

If I was filling this in for myself I would choose my ambition as a talent, my kindness to animals as a talent, my photographic long-term memory is a talent, my loyalty to my job is a talent.

MY BIGGEST FEARS

I know, I know: it's cruel to ask someone what their biggest fears are, after all, our biggest fears could be used against us (but this book is only being shared with trusted, safe adults so it's a safe place to write everything down). I will go first and share mine.

As anyone who buys this journal will know, I am much older and can just hop in my car and drive away if anyone tries to scare me...well, sort of! MOTORWAYS are one of my biggest fears!! I don't mind being in somebody else's car, with someone else driving on a motorway, but ME driving on an actual motorway? Absolutely not, thank you! Too fast, terrible signage, no idea where I am – it makes me want to vomit!

Second to motorways? The sea! I can just about put my feet in the sea on holiday, but I can hear the *Jaws* movie music (dum, dum dum dum) playing in my mind and convince myself that the seaweed is a great white shark about to gobble me up.

My fear of the sea is so bad that I once went into meltdown on a pier. I wasn't even close to the sea itself, I was above it, but it seemed so big, deep, uncertain, unpredictable, argh!

Ok, last but by no means least: being late. I hate being late and letting people down. I think that if I can't be early I may as well not turn up at all; after all, you can't be late if you didn't show up, right?

So why ask what your fears are, is it helpful? Actually, yes! Knowing our fears can help us have a day, week or month filled with things that we are not scared to say "yes" to. It can help our trusted adults better support us.

Will my parents and grown-up children ever expect me to take a stroll down a pier again? Nope!

Will my friends understand why I can't just whizz down the motorway to visit them and instead will need to ask them to visit me, arrange for a lift or ask for extra time to take the train? Yes!

Will they also know the extra time is super important to me as if I am going to run late, I'd rather cancel? Yes again. So go ahead and jot down your fears!

(Side note: many people say "just get over your fears!" I say: don't. Love your fears. After all, if I was "cured" of my fear of being late, I'd be much less likely to be known as the person who is reliable and always in work on time.)

MY FAVOURITE ANIMALS

Animals can be a huge source of comfort for Autistic people. Many of the Autistic young people I have supported over the last 14 years have even brought their pets to show me.

We have had snakes, talking parrots, snails, cats, dogs and more turn up to say hi. Luckily nobody has had a pet tiger yet, but if they did and it was a tame tiger I guess that would be cool?

In our family we have a specially trained Autism assistance dog called Hunter (not sure if the name suits though as he tends to only hunt tennis balls and cheese).

I have this dream of one day earning enough money to buy a farm (which is daft really as I am not good with bad smells!). The farm would be called "D Farm" as every animal there would begin with the letter D. Dogs, Deer, Ducks, Donkeys.

What would your farm, zoo, aquarium be filled with? What pets do you have? Which pet would you like to have one day? What animals make you feel calm, or excited and happy to be around?

IF I COULD BE IN ANY BOOK, FILM OR PLAY I'D BE...

So here's the thing, I wrote this part into the journal thinking that the person filling it out (that's you by the way) would have an interest in books, film and theatre. You may not though, which is absolutely fine! In that case think about any fiction (made-up) thing you like.

My family love books and movies. So we often like to play this game. It's fun and also helps us understand how we see ourselves, see the world around us and see our own life experiences in fictional media. There haven't been too many Autistic people young and not so young represented in the media BUT there are characters that we can identify with.

My answers would be (and always are): Book? Susanna Kaysen from *Girl, Interrupted*. Film? Bridget Jones in *Bridget Jones' Diary* (the first one NOT the second or third film) and Nancy from *Oliver!* (the musical).

Who and what would yours be? Have fun with it! Maybe the character you'd most like to be hasn't appeared in a book, film, or play yet? If so, write it! The world needs to read, see and find out more about what you have to share!

IF I COULD HAVE WRITTEN ANY SONG IT WOULD BE...

Here I go again being "Autistic and Artistic". (I am sure the words are similar for a reason!) Songs are a great way to share how we are feeling with others and, more importantly, with ourselves It could be a sad song with serious lyrics; it could be just the beat, energy or feel-good nature of a happy song.

Later in the journal you'll be able to add a song of the day – after all, it's our most listened to songs change with our moods and experiences.

WHAT I LIKE MOST IN OTHER PEOPLE...

Sometimes if life feels tough, it's hard to remember all the beautiful things that people do, or even to remember that there are amazing humans out there! If we write a list of the things we like in other humans it can help us remember that good humans exist. It can help us look out for the type of humans who make us feel happy, safe and valued in the future and help our trusted adults know what qualities in other humans (including them!) make our life happier and easier.

WHAT I LIKE LEAST IN OTHER PEOPLE...

This is your venting space! It's a place to write down all the things that really annoy you about other humans. It will hopefully help you move away from situations and "friends" that aren't good for your happiness, and it can help your loved ones and safe adults recognize what you really don't want from other people!

IF I COULD MAKE ONE NEW LAW IT WOULD BE...

This doesn't need to be serious, but it can be if you have a burning passion for a cause or a change you desperately want to see in the world. If not, it could just be "chocolate is free on Sundays" or "everyone gets a free puppy when they turn 13".

This question gives you a chance to reflect on what is really important to you. (Puppies and chocolate are very important, obviously!)

ALL ABOUT TODAY

All about today is a page for each day to write down the best and worst things that happened. It is a good way to remember our day in a more personal way than on social media. It's also a great way to protect ourselves by allowing our trusted loved ones and safe adults to see when things may be difficult for us to manage without support and understanding.

Writing down the weather may seem odd! Being British I do like to talk about the weather a lot, but there's more to it than that. If you notice that you are having happier days when there's a certain type of weather, it can help you to understand your sensory needs, think about what you need and plan ahead.

Same idea when it comes to writing down our favourite meal of the day: it can help us remember what foods we really enjoy for days when eating feels like a chore, can remind us to eat if we become busy with our special interests and activities, can help us think forward to tomorrow and plan our meals.

If our trusted loved ones and safe adults know our favourite foods, it can help them order and buy the right things in the food shop – which means everyone is less likely to be upset at meal times! If they don't know what we like they can't help us stay healthy.

THE BEST THING THAT HAPPENED TODAY...

The best thing doesn't have to be something huge and exciting, it could be something tiny that made you happy or it may have been someone's birthday and seeing them happy was the best thing.

Every day has something that's the "best" and, even if it's the worst day you feel you have ever had, maybe the best thing could be that you got through the day. I really hope there are many huge, medium and small best things for you.

THE WORST THING THAT HAPPENED TODAY...

Much like the best thing that happened in a day, even the most amazing days have something that wasn't as great as the rest. Some days the worst things will be huge, some days medium, some days small.

I hope your "worst" things aren't too awful, but if they are, write them down so you and your safe trusted adults know what has happened straight away. If something very difficult happens, keeping a record of it will help the people around you to remember you might need extra support on that date in the future.

THE WEATHER WAS...

Some Autistic people feel overwhelmed on sunny days, even though everyone else is saying it's a lovely day. If you are sensitive to light, the sun can be overwhelming.

The days are longer in the summer and there are often expectations to go to more family or educational events. BBQs, parties, etc can all get a bit much.

Many Autistic people prefer the winter and cosy days in and it can be helpful to know this. We are all different though, with different likes, so be creative and write or draw the weather of the day.

MY FAVE MEAL WAS...

Write your favourite meal of the day here. You could even write what your "dream meal" of the day would have been if it were available. (Mine would be sushi and Rum and Rasin ice-cream – not eaten together, obviously, that would be gross.)

IF TODAY HAD A SOUNDTRACK IT WOULD BE...

Pick the song or songs that best describe your day. If your day had been filmed as part of a film or TV show what would the background music have been?

ALL ABOUT THIS WEEK

At the end of each week is an "all about this week" page to fill in. You can use this space to look back on the week that has happened and look forward, plan and get ready for the week ahead. This can help us be mentally ready for what is about to come, let go of the week that has passed and, if you are sharing your journal with trusted safe adults, it can help them to know what is really exciting and important for you next week so they can do their best to make sure things aren't cancelled. It can also show them what you are worried and anxious about, so they can support you more.

THE GOOD...

Write or draw here all the good things that were in your "best thing" of the day. Are there more best things now a few days have passed that you want to add?

THE BAD...

Write or draw here the worst things of the week just past. Are there more or fewer things to add when you look back?

THE NEUTRAL

There are things in our weeks which don't neatly fit into "good" or "bad". Some things are just things, but you may want to write them down too. Use this space for those things that just are things!

NEXT WEEK I AM LOOKING FORWARD TO...

Is there anything coming up next week that is super important and exciting for you? What would be most disappointing if it was cancelled or couldn't happen? Write or draw it here.

MY BIGGEST CHALLENGE NEXT WEEK

Every week has a challenge. That's not always a bad thing: we grow by experiencing new challenges. They can be scary or make us anxious before they happen though, and that's totally natural! Write or draw the challenge that next week brings here.

MESSAGE TO MYSELF FOR THIS TIME NEXT WEEK

I once heard that organization is being your own future best friend. Let's say you needed a shirt that was cleaned and ironed for early Monday morning. What would your best friend do for you on Sunday? They'd iron your shirt for you! In the same way, let's say you had a dentist appointment you were scared of on Monday afternoon, what would your best friend write in a letter for you to open? Be your own best friend here! Write a letter to you FROM you and read it when you need to over the upcoming week.

QUOTES

You will notice that in your journal there are quotes, messages and advice from other people. Some of these people you may have heard of, some you may not.

These quotes have been kindly sent to me from other Autistic adults who wanted to share the things they wished they had known when they were younger, or from parents and professionals who support Autistic people of all ages and had kind and helpful things they wanted to share with you.

Some quotes you may agree with, some you may not, and that's ok. Maybe consider what you would have told yourself a year, five years or even longer ago? What do you know now that you wish you had known when you were younger?

Why not write your own quote or advice to your younger self here?

MY JOURNAL

ALL ABOUT ME!

HELLO MY NAME IS:

AGE:

ME!

MY BIGGEST TALENTS:

MY BIGGEST FEARS:

MY FAVOURITE ANIMALS:

IN A TV OR FILM, I'D LIKE TO PLAY:

IF I COULD HAVE WRITTEN ANY SONG IT WOULD BE:

THE WORLD NEEDS:

MORE...

LESS...

IF I COULD MAKE ONE NEW LAW IT WOULD BE:

ALL ABOUT TODAY __/__/__

THE BEST THING

THE WORST THING

THE WEATHER WAS:

MY FAVE MEAL WAS:

IF TODAY HAD A SOUNDTRACK THE SONG WOULD BE:

ALL ABOUT TODAY __ / __ / __

THE BEST THING

THE WORST THING

THE WEATHER WAS:

MY FAVE MEAL WAS:

IF TODAY HAD A SOUNDTRACK THE SONG WOULD BE:

ALL ABOUT TODAY __/__/__

THE BEST THING

THE WORST THING

THE WEATHER WAS:

MY FAVE MEAL WAS:

IF TODAY HAD A SOUNDTRACK THE SONG WOULD BE:

ALL ABOUT TODAY __/__/__

THE BEST THING

THE WORST THING

THE WEATHER WAS:

MY FAVE MEAL WAS:

IF TODAY HAD A SOUNDTRACK THE SONG WOULD BE:

ALL ABOUT TODAY __/__/__

THE BEST THING

THE WORST THING

THE WEATHER WAS:

MY FAVE MEAL WAS:

IF TODAY HAD A SOUNDTRACK THE SONG WOULD BE:

ALL ABOUT TODAY__/__/__

THE BEST THING

THE WORST THING

THE WEATHER WAS:

MY FAVE MEAL WAS:

IF TODAY HAD A SOUNDTRACK THE SONG WOULD BE:

ALL ABOUT TODAY __/__/__

THE BEST THING

THE WORST THING

THE WEATHER WAS:

MY FAVE MEAL WAS:

IF TODAY HAD A SOUNDTRACK THE SONG WOULD BE:

"Sometimes people are drawn to, and like people who are different to them. So calm people may seek out busy people, funny people maybe drawn to sad, and so on.

As hard as it is, try to stay YOU because that's where the magic is and where you'll attract the right people in your life."

— CARLY X

ALL ABOUT THIS WEEK

MON __/__/__ TO SUN __/__/__

THE GOOD!

THE BAD...

THE NEUTRAL.

NEXT WEEK I'M LOOKING FORWARD TO:

MY BIGGEST CHALLENGE NEXT WEEK:

MESSAGE TO MYSELF FOR THIS TIME NEXT WEEK:

"If you mask around other people in order to try and fit in, take the time to stop and think about what relationships are healthy. Are these relationships helping you or making you feel better?"

– CARLY X

ALL ABOUT TODAY __/__/__

THE BEST THING

THE WORST THING

THE WEATHER WAS:

MY FAVE MEAL WAS:

IF TODAY HAD A SOUNDTRACK THE SONG WOULD BE:

ALL ABOUT TODAY __/__/__

THE BEST THING

THE WORST THING

THE WEATHER WAS:

MY FAVE MEAL WAS:

IF TODAY HAD A SOUNDTRACK THE SONG WOULD BE:

ALL ABOUT TODAY __/__/__

THE BEST THING

THE WORST THING

THE WEATHER WAS:

MY FAVE MEAL WAS:

IF TODAY HAD A SOUNDTRACK THE SONG WOULD BE:

ALL ABOUT TODAY __/__/__

THE BEST THING

THE WORST THING

THE WEATHER WAS:

MY FAVE MEAL WAS:

IF TODAY HAD A SOUNDTRACK THE SONG WOULD BE:

ALL ABOUT TODAY __/__/__

THE BEST THING

THE WORST THING

THE WEATHER WAS:

MY FAVE MEAL WAS:

IF TODAY HAD A SOUNDTRACK THE SONG WOULD BE:

ALL ABOUT TODAY __/__/__

THE BEST THING

THE WORST THING

THE WEATHER WAS:

MY FAVE MEAL WAS:

IF TODAY HAD A SOUNDTRACK THE SONG WOULD BE:

ALL ABOUT TODAY __/__/__

THE BEST THING

THE WORST THING

THE WEATHER WAS:

MY FAVE MEAL WAS:

IF TODAY HAD A SOUNDTRACK THE SONG WOULD BE:

"WORK YOUR BUTT OFF! AS MY DAD TOLD ME, NO PAIN NO GAIN, BUT GIVE BACK TIME WITH FAMILY, FRIENDS AND HELP SUPPORT OTHERS. BE STRONG."

– OLIVER MCGOWAN

Oliver McGowan was an Autistic teenager. He died in tragic circumstances in 2016 when he was given the wrong medication in hospital, against his and his parents' will. This quote was written by Oliver before he died and kindly provided by his mother, Paula McGowan OBE.

You can find out more about Oliver's story and Paula's campaigning at: https://www.olivermcgowan.org.

ALL ABOUT THIS WEEK

MON __/__/__ TO SUN __/__/__

THE GOOD!

THE BAD...

THE NEUTRAL.

NEXT WEEK I'M LOOKING FORWARD TO:

MY BIGGEST CHALLENGE NEXT WEEK:

MESSAGE TO MYSELF FOR THIS TIME NEXT WEEK:

"It took me seven driving tests and three years of lessons to pass my driving test. It's always good to persevere if there's something you really want to achieve."

- CARLY X

"Even when you hit your lowest, when there seems no help and the right people won't listen. Keep going, and if going means doing nothing that's ok, because it does get better. Xxx"

– Tanya Newing

Tanya Newing, SEN residential support worker and mother of two young adults with sen.

ALL ABOUT TODAY __/__/__

THE BEST THING

THE WORST THING

THE WEATHER WAS:

MY FAVE MEAL WAS:

IF TODAY HAD A SOUNDTRACK THE SONG WOULD BE:

ALL ABOUT TODAY __/__/__

THE BEST THING

THE WORST THING

THE WEATHER WAS:

MY FAVE MEAL WAS:

IF TODAY HAD A SOUNDTRACK THE SONG WOULD BE:

ALL ABOUT TODAY __/__/__

THE BEST THING

THE WORST THING

THE WEATHER WAS:

MY FAVE MEAL WAS:

IF TODAY HAD A SOUNDTRACK THE SONG WOULD BE:

ALL ABOUT TODAY __/__/__

THE BEST THING

THE WORST THING

THE WEATHER WAS:

MY FAVE MEAL WAS:

IF TODAY HAD A SOUNDTRACK THE SONG WOULD BE:

ALL ABOUT TODAY __/__/__

THE BEST THING

THE WORST THING

THE WEATHER WAS:

MY FAVE MEAL WAS:

IF TODAY HAD A SOUNDTRACK THE SONG WOULD BE:

ALL ABOUT TODAY __/__/__

THE BEST THING

THE WORST THING

THE WEATHER WAS:

MY FAVE MEAL WAS:

IF TODAY HAD A SOUNDTRACK THE SONG WOULD BE:

ALL ABOUT TODAY __/__/__

THE BEST THING

THE WORST THING

THE WEATHER WAS:

MY FAVE MEAL WAS:

IF TODAY HAD A SOUNDTRACK THE SONG WOULD BE:

"THE OLDER I GOT THE MORE
I SPOTTED A PATTERN: THE
NAMES THAT PEOPLE CALLED ME
WHETHER THEY WERE KIND OR
VERY UNKIND WERE ACTUALLY A
REFLECTION OF HOW THEY
FELT ABOUT THEMSELVES.

THE WAY WE TREAT OTHERS
ALSO SAYS A LOT ABOUT HOW
WE SEE OURSELVES."

— CARLY X

ALL ABOUT THIS WEEK

MON __/__/__ TO SUN __/__/__

THE GOOD!

THE BAD...

THE NEUTRAL.

NEXT WEEK I'M LOOKING FORWARD TO:

MY BIGGEST CHALLENGE NEXT WEEK:

MESSAGE TO MYSELF FOR THIS TIME NEXT WEEK:

"Ignore the negative thoughts you can't change, but change the negative things you can't ignore."

– Oliver McGowan

Oliver McGowan was an Autistic teenager. He died in tragic circumstances in 2016 when he was given the wrong medication in hospital, against his and his parents' will. This quote was written by Oliver before he died and kindly provided by his mother, Paula McGowan OBE.

You can find out more about Oliver's story and Paula's campaigning at: https://www.olivermcgowan.org.

"Having time alone is ok. Some people have their battery recharged by being around lots of other people, some people feel fully charged after being on their own for a while and both are ok."

- CARLY X

ALL ABOUT TODAY __/__/__

THE BEST THING

THE WORST THING

THE WEATHER WAS:

MY FAVE MEAL WAS:

IF TODAY HAD A SOUNDTRACK THE SONG WOULD BE:

ALL ABOUT TODAY __/__/__

THE BEST THING

THE WORST THING

THE WEATHER WAS:

MY FAVE MEAL WAS:

IF TODAY HAD A SOUNDTRACK THE SONG WOULD BE:

ALL ABOUT TODAY __/__/__

THE BEST THING

THE WORST THING

THE WEATHER WAS:

MY FAVE MEAL WAS:

IF TODAY HAD A SOUNDTRACK THE SONG WOULD BE:

ALL ABOUT TODAY __/__/__

THE BEST THING

THE WORST THING

THE WEATHER WAS:

MY FAVE MEAL WAS:

IF TODAY HAD A SOUNDTRACK THE SONG WOULD BE:

ALL ABOUT TODAY __/__/__

THE BEST THING

THE WORST THING

THE WEATHER WAS:

MY FAVE MEAL WAS:

IF TODAY HAD A SOUNDTRACK THE SONG WOULD BE:

ALL ABOUT TODAY __/__/__

THE BEST THING

THE WORST THING

THE WEATHER WAS:

MY FAVE MEAL WAS:

IF TODAY HAD A SOUNDTRACK THE SONG WOULD BE:

ALL ABOUT TODAY __/__/__

THE BEST THING

THE WORST THING

THE WEATHER WAS:

MY FAVE MEAL WAS:

IF TODAY HAD A SOUNDTRACK THE SONG WOULD BE:

ALL ABOUT THIS WEEK

MON __/__/__ TO SUN __/__/__

THE GOOD!

THE BAD...

THE NEUTRAL.

NEXT WEEK I'M LOOKING FORWARD TO:

MY BIGGEST CHALLENGE NEXT WEEK:

MESSAGE TO MYSELF FOR THIS TIME NEXT WEEK:

"IF I HAD ONE BIT OF ADVICE TO MY YOUNGER SELF IT WOULD BE STOP BENDING YOUR ARMS AND LEGS AS A FUNNY PARTY TRICK! YOU ARE HYPERMOBILE AND IT WILL REALLY ACHE WHEN YOU'RE OLDER! "

- CARLY X

"If you're struggling with some self-care because of sensory input, it's absolutely ok to brush teeth in bed because the cold bathroom floor puts you off."

– Kelly Harmer-Jones

Kelly is originally from North Wales but now lives in Berkshire. She is a development chef and mum. She was diagnosed Autistic in her 30s and has since gone on a long journey of discovery to find out what the diagnosis means for her, and to practise being kinder to herself.

ALL ABOUT TODAY __/__/__

THE BEST THING

THE WORST THING

THE WEATHER WAS:

MY FAVE MEAL WAS:

IF TODAY HAD A SOUNDTRACK THE SONG WOULD BE:

ALL ABOUT TODAY __/__/__

THE BEST THING

THE WORST THING

THE WEATHER WAS:

MY FAVE MEAL WAS:

IF TODAY HAD A SOUNDTRACK THE SONG WOULD BE:

ALL ABOUT TODAY __/__/__

THE BEST THING

THE WORST THING

THE WEATHER WAS:

MY FAVE MEAL WAS:

IF TODAY HAD A SOUNDTRACK THE SONG WOULD BE:

ALL ABOUT TODAY __/__/__

THE BEST THING

THE WORST THING

THE WEATHER WAS:

MY FAVE MEAL WAS:

IF TODAY HAD A SOUNDTRACK THE SONG WOULD BE:

ALL ABOUT TODAY __/__/__

THE BEST THING

THE WORST THING

THE WEATHER WAS:

MY FAVE MEAL WAS:

IF TODAY HAD A SOUNDTRACK THE SONG WOULD BE:

ALL ABOUT TODAY __/__/__

THE BEST THING

THE WORST THING

THE WEATHER WAS:

MY FAVE MEAL WAS:

IF TODAY HAD A SOUNDTRACK THE SONG WOULD BE:

ALL ABOUT TODAY __/__/__

THE BEST THING

THE WORST THING

THE WEATHER WAS:

MY FAVE MEAL WAS:

IF TODAY HAD A SOUNDTRACK THE SONG WOULD BE:

"Having a clear sense of justice and feeling strongly about what is right and wrong often won't win you many friends when younger, but as an adult it's a rare skill needed in some top professions."

- CARLY X

ALL ABOUT THIS WEEK

MON __/__/__ TO SUN __/__/__

THE GOOD!

THE BAD...

THE NEUTRAL.

NEXT WEEK I'M LOOKING FORWARD TO:

MY BIGGEST CHALLENGE NEXT WEEK:

MESSAGE TO MYSELF FOR THIS TIME NEXT WEEK:

"I ONCE READ THAT YOU DON'T HAVE TO BE GOOD AT SOMETHING TO ENJOY IT. THERE IS A LOT OF PRESSURE TO BE THE BEST AT SOMETHING IF WE SPEND A LOT OF TIME DOING IT.

I SAY: DON'T TRY TO BE THE BEST AT SOMETHING, JUST ENJOY IT AND STICK TO YOUR INDIVIDUAL WAY OF WRITING, DRAWING, PAINTING, WHATEVER IT IS YOU DO – AS LONG AS YOU'RE HAVING FUN IT'S NEVER TIME WASTED IS IT?"

– CARLY X

"Growing up, I often felt out of place or as though I had done something wrong. I still feel like this sometimes, but I know now that it isn't my fault.

People sometimes react to me in an unhelpful way because of prejudice and I can't control that, but I can control whether I allow them to upset me, or whether I keep them in my life. Since I started putting myself first more, I've had more energy to devote to things I'm passionate about."

– Sarah McHaffie

Sara McHaffie is a PhD student and associate lecturer at Northumbria University. The working title for her thesis is 'Co-producing articulations of autistic women's feminist consciousness'. She is also a trainer. Before embarking on her PhD, she worked in the women's sector, particularly with women who experience multiple forms of marginalization.

ALL ABOUT TODAY __/__/__

THE BEST THING

THE WORST THING

THE WEATHER WAS:

MY FAVE MEAL WAS:

IF TODAY HAD A SOUNDTRACK THE SONG WOULD BE:

ALL ABOUT TODAY __/__/__

THE BEST THING

THE WORST THING

THE WEATHER WAS:

MY FAVE MEAL WAS:

IF TODAY HAD A SOUNDTRACK THE SONG WOULD BE:

ALL ABOUT TODAY __/__/__

THE BEST THING

THE WORST THING

THE WEATHER WAS:

MY FAVE MEAL WAS:

IF TODAY HAD A SOUNDTRACK THE SONG WOULD BE:

ALL ABOUT TODAY __/__/__

THE BEST THING

THE WORST THING

THE WEATHER WAS:

MY FAVE MEAL WAS:

IF TODAY HAD A SOUNDTRACK THE SONG WOULD BE:

ALL ABOUT TODAY __/__/__

THE BEST THING

THE WORST THING

THE WEATHER WAS:

MY FAVE MEAL WAS:

IF TODAY HAD A SOUNDTRACK THE SONG WOULD BE:

ALL ABOUT TODAY __/__/__

THE BEST THING

THE WORST THING

THE WEATHER WAS:

MY FAVE MEAL WAS:

IF TODAY HAD A SOUNDTRACK THE SONG WOULD BE:

ALL ABOUT TODAY __/__/__

THE BEST THING

THE WORST THING

THE WEATHER WAS:

MY FAVE MEAL WAS:

IF TODAY HAD A SOUNDTRACK THE SONG WOULD BE:

"If you are going somewhere and not feeling confident write three things that you like about yourself and read it before you go. It will give you confidence."

– Dawn Seabright

Dawn is an Autistic advocate who has worked with people with disabilities for many years. She has presented several radio shows for family members or friends who are carers and is a parent and grandparent to Autistic children and Autistic grandchildren!

ALL ABOUT THIS WEEK

MON __/__/__ TO SUN __/__/__

THE GOOD!

THE BAD...

THE NEUTRAL.

NEXT WEEK I'M LOOKING FORWARD TO:

MY BIGGEST CHALLENGE NEXT WEEK:

MESSAGE TO MYSELF FOR THIS TIME NEXT WEEK:

"ANIMALS OFFER THE BEST TYPE OF FRIENDSHIP FOR AUTISTIC PEOPLE. THEY ARE HAPPY TO SIT IN SILENCE WITH YOU WHEN YOU HAVE NO WORDS TO SAY. THEY DON'T JUDGE YOU WHEN YOU DO TALK. THEY DON'T CARE WHAT HAIRCUT YOU'VE GOT, IF YOU ARE DRESSED UP OR IN YOUR TRACKSUIT FOR THREE DAYS RUNNING.

SOMETIMES I WISH HUMANS WERE MORE LIKE ANIMALS."

– CARLY X

"As someone who has worried all my life, this is what I'd have liked to be told: It's not unusual to worry, to think too much about a situation/task, or to look at a situation/task without panicking. What IS important is that you take a minute to breathe/do mindfulness/exercise/stim etc.

Once you're ready, consider - is it worth worrying about, can you break a task down into chunks with breaks in between, can anyone help you, is it THAT important? The reality is you are not being judged and you can ask for help, it's OK."

– Sarah Weston

Sarah's job is to signpost/guide under 19s (and their families) experiencing emotional wellbeing challenges to the most appropriate support. She is a married mum of two ND teens, with a pet cat and a tortoise, who is navigating her way through a late autism diagnosis, parenting teens and menopause!

ALL ABOUT TODAY __/__/__

THE BEST THING

THE WORST THING

THE WEATHER WAS:

MY FAVE MEAL WAS:

IF TODAY HAD A SOUNDTRACK THE SONG WOULD BE:

ALL ABOUT TODAY __/__/__

THE BEST THING

THE WORST THING

THE WEATHER WAS:

MY FAVE MEAL WAS:

IF TODAY HAD A SOUNDTRACK THE SONG WOULD BE:

ALL ABOUT TODAY __/__/__

THE BEST THING

THE WORST THING

THE WEATHER WAS:

MY FAVE MEAL WAS:

IF TODAY HAD A SOUNDTRACK THE SONG WOULD BE:

ALL ABOUT TODAY__/__/__

THE BEST THING

THE WORST THING

THE WEATHER WAS:

MY FAVE MEAL WAS:

IF TODAY HAD A SOUNDTRACK THE SONG WOULD BE:

ALL ABOUT TODAY __/__/__

THE BEST THING

THE WORST THING

THE WEATHER WAS:

MY FAVE MEAL WAS:

IF TODAY HAD A SOUNDTRACK THE SONG WOULD BE:

ALL ABOUT TODAY __/__/__

THE BEST THING

THE WORST THING

THE WEATHER WAS:

MY FAVE MEAL WAS:

IF TODAY HAD A SOUNDTRACK THE SONG WOULD BE:

ALL ABOUT TODAY __/__/__

THE BEST THING

THE WORST THING

THE WEATHER WAS:

MY FAVE MEAL WAS:

IF TODAY HAD A SOUNDTRACK THE SONG WOULD BE:

"To save embarrassing situations, always pay careful attention to jargon and stock phrases on invitations. I once bought a black tie to wear for a black tie event as I didn't know what 'black tie event' meant.

Even worse, when my children were small their school sent out an invite for the class to bring a parent to a Pyjamas and Movie night in the school hall one Friday evening. I was the only parent also in pyjamas! If you need more context or have questions about an event, always ask!"

– CARLY X

ALL ABOUT THIS WEEK

MON __/__/__ TO SUN __/__/__

THE GOOD!

THE BAD...

THE NEUTRAL.

NEXT WEEK I'M LOOKING FORWARD TO:

MY BIGGEST CHALLENGE NEXT WEEK:

MESSAGE TO MYSELF FOR THIS TIME NEXT WEEK:

"YOU COULD BE THE
MOST DELICIOUS JUICY
STRAWBERRY IN THE WORLD,
STILL SOMEONE
WOULD HATE STRAWBERRIES."

– KELLY HARMER-JONES

Kelly is originally from North Wales but now lives in
Berkshire. She is a development chef and mum.
She was diagnosed Autistic in her 30s and has since
gone on a long journey of discovery to find out what
the diagnosis means for her, and to practise being
kinder to herself.

"If it is Sunday and someone says they'll see you next Wednesday do they mean they'll see you in three days' time or the Wednesday in the NEXT week (so in 10 days' time)? Why can't everyone just talk in calendar dates?!

Always feel confident to check on details if you're not sure about something."

- CARLY X

ALL ABOUT TODAY __/__/__

THE BEST THING

THE WORST THING

THE WEATHER WAS:

MY FAVE MEAL WAS:

IF TODAY HAD A SOUNDTRACK THE SONG WOULD BE:

ALL ABOUT TODAY __/__/__

THE BEST THING

THE WORST THING

THE WEATHER WAS:

MY FAVE MEAL WAS:

IF TODAY HAD A SOUNDTRACK THE SONG WOULD BE:

ALL ABOUT TODAY __/__/__

THE BEST THING

THE WORST THING

THE WEATHER WAS:

MY FAVE MEAL WAS:

IF TODAY HAD A SOUNDTRACK THE SONG WOULD BE:

ALL ABOUT TODAY __/__/__

THE BEST THING

THE WORST THING

THE WEATHER WAS:

MY FAVE MEAL WAS:

IF TODAY HAD A SOUNDTRACK THE SONG WOULD BE:

ALL ABOUT TODAY __/__/__

THE BEST THING

THE WORST THING

THE WEATHER WAS:

MY FAVE MEAL WAS:

IF TODAY HAD A SOUNDTRACK THE SONG WOULD BE:

ALL ABOUT TODAY __/__/__

THE BEST THING

THE WORST THING

THE WEATHER WAS:

MY FAVE MEAL WAS:

IF TODAY HAD A SOUNDTRACK THE SONG WOULD BE:

ALL ABOUT TODAY __/__/__

THE BEST THING

THE WORST THING

THE WEATHER WAS:

MY FAVE MEAL WAS:

IF TODAY HAD A SOUNDTRACK THE SONG WOULD BE:

ALL ABOUT THIS WEEK

MON __/__/__ TO SUN __/__/__

THE GOOD!

THE BAD...

THE NEUTRAL.

NEXT WEEK I'M LOOKING FORWARD TO:

MY BIGGEST CHALLENGE NEXT WEEK:

MESSAGE TO MYSELF FOR THIS TIME NEXT WEEK:

"IT'S OK TO BE QUIRKY!"

– JAN KILEY

Jan is Operations Manager for Dogs for Autism, and a qualified primary school teacher. She works to connect families with dogs who will best meet their needs.

"If you're having a bad day with zero motivation but a much needed duvet day isn't possible, remember some days we have to get motivated before we can get started and some days we need to get started before we can feel motivated. Get started and see what happens."

- CARLY X

ALL ABOUT TODAY __/__/__

THE BEST THING

THE WORST THING

THE WEATHER WAS:

MY FAVE MEAL WAS:

IF TODAY HAD A SOUNDTRACK THE SONG WOULD BE:

ALL ABOUT TODAY __/__/__

THE BEST THING

THE WORST THING

THE WEATHER WAS:

MY FAVE MEAL WAS:

IF TODAY HAD A SOUNDTRACK THE SONG WOULD BE:

ALL ABOUT TODAY __/__/__

THE BEST THING

THE WORST THING

THE WEATHER WAS:

MY FAVE MEAL WAS:

IF TODAY HAD A SOUNDTRACK THE SONG WOULD BE:

ALL ABOUT TODAY__/__/__

THE BEST THING

THE WORST THING

THE WEATHER WAS:

MY FAVE MEAL WAS:

IF TODAY HAD A SOUNDTRACK THE SONG WOULD BE:

ALL ABOUT TODAY __/__/__

THE BEST THING

THE WORST THING

THE WEATHER WAS:

MY FAVE MEAL WAS:

IF TODAY HAD A SOUNDTRACK THE SONG WOULD BE:

ALL ABOUT TODAY __/__/__

THE BEST THING

THE WORST THING

THE WEATHER WAS:

MY FAVE MEAL WAS:

IF TODAY HAD A SOUNDTRACK THE SONG WOULD BE:

ALL ABOUT TODAY __/__/__

THE BEST THING

THE WORST THING

THE WEATHER WAS:

MY FAVE MEAL WAS:

IF TODAY HAD A SOUNDTRACK THE SONG WOULD BE:

"Nothing hits harder than reality. It can come at the worst of times which is why it's important to have a strong mentality. Find the good that's hidden between the lines. Expect the worst when you hope for the best. Have self respect and be understanding because you don't want to be like everyone else.

Keep knowledge expanding. Never let failure become something stronger. Embrace your mistakes like it's your mentor. Change negatives to a positive."

– Oliver McGowan

Oliver McGowan was an autistic teenager, who died in tragic circumstances in 2016 when he was given the wrong medication in hospital, against his and his parents' will. This quote was written by Oliver before he died and have been kindly provided by his mother, Paula McGowan OBE.

You can find out more about Oliver's story and Paula's campaigning at: https://www.olivermcgowan.org.

ALL ABOUT THIS WEEK

MON __/__/__ TO SUN __/__/__

THE GOOD!

THE BAD...

THE NEUTRAL.

NEXT WEEK I'M LOOKING FORWARD TO:

MY BIGGEST CHALLENGE NEXT WEEK:

MESSAGE TO MYSELF FOR THIS TIME NEXT WEEK:

"YOU DON'T OWE ANYONE
THE MOST PERSONAL AND
PRIVATE STORIES OF YOUR
LIFE JUST SO THEY BELIEVE
YOU'RE AUTISTIC."

– CARLY X

ALL ABOUT TODAY __/__/__

THE BEST THING

THE WORST THING

THE WEATHER WAS:

MY FAVE MEAL WAS:

IF TODAY HAD A SOUNDTRACK THE SONG WOULD BE:

ALL ABOUT TODAY __/__/__

THE BEST THING

THE WORST THING

THE WEATHER WAS:

MY FAVE MEAL WAS:

IF TODAY HAD A SOUNDTRACK THE SONG WOULD BE:

ALL ABOUT TODAY __/__/__

THE BEST THING

THE WORST THING

THE WEATHER WAS:

MY FAVE MEAL WAS:

IF TODAY HAD A SOUNDTRACK THE SONG WOULD BE:

ALL ABOUT TODAY __/__/__

THE BEST THING

THE WORST THING

THE WEATHER WAS:

MY FAVE MEAL WAS:

IF TODAY HAD A SOUNDTRACK THE SONG WOULD BE:

ALL ABOUT TODAY __/__/__

THE BEST THING

THE WORST THING

THE WEATHER WAS:

MY FAVE MEAL WAS:

IF TODAY HAD A SOUNDTRACK THE SONG WOULD BE:

ALL ABOUT TODAY __/__/__

THE BEST THING

THE WORST THING

THE WEATHER WAS:

MY FAVE MEAL WAS:

IF TODAY HAD A SOUNDTRACK THE SONG WOULD BE:

ALL ABOUT TODAY __/__/__

THE BEST THING

THE WORST THING

THE WEATHER WAS:

MY FAVE MEAL WAS:

IF TODAY HAD A SOUNDTRACK THE SONG WOULD BE:

"I like old cities. I get lost a lot when cities change. Old cities have rooftops that rarely change. If you're lost, literally keep your chin up until you remember where you are."

- CARLY X

ALL ABOUT THIS WEEK

MON __/__/__ TO SUN __/__/__

THE GOOD!

THE BAD...

THE NEUTRAL.

NEXT WEEK I'M LOOKING FORWARD TO:

MY BIGGEST CHALLENGE NEXT WEEK:

MESSAGE TO MYSELF FOR THIS TIME NEXT WEEK:

ALL ABOUT TODAY __/__/__

THE BEST THING

THE WORST THING

THE WEATHER WAS:

MY FAVE MEAL WAS:

IF TODAY HAD A SOUNDTRACK THE SONG WOULD BE:

ALL ABOUT TODAY __/__/__

THE BEST THING

THE WORST THING

THE WEATHER WAS:

MY FAVE MEAL WAS:

IF TODAY HAD A SOUNDTRACK THE SONG WOULD BE:

ALL ABOUT TODAY __/__/__

THE BEST THING

THE WORST THING

THE WEATHER WAS:

MY FAVE MEAL WAS:

IF TODAY HAD A SOUNDTRACK THE SONG WOULD BE:

ALL ABOUT TODAY__/__/__

THE BEST THING

THE WORST THING

THE WEATHER WAS:

MY FAVE MEAL WAS:

IF TODAY HAD A SOUNDTRACK THE SONG WOULD BE:

ALL ABOUT TODAY __/__/__

THE BEST THING

THE WORST THING

THE WEATHER WAS:

MY FAVE MEAL WAS:

IF TODAY HAD A SOUNDTRACK THE SONG WOULD BE:

ALL ABOUT TODAY __/__/__

THE BEST THING

THE WORST THING

THE WEATHER WAS:

MY FAVE MEAL WAS:

IF TODAY HAD A SOUNDTRACK THE SONG WOULD BE:

ALL ABOUT TODAY __/__/__

THE BEST THING

THE WORST THING

THE WEATHER WAS:

MY FAVE MEAL WAS:

IF TODAY HAD A SOUNDTRACK THE SONG WOULD BE:

"Be yourself :)"

— CARLY X

ALL ABOUT THIS WEEK

MON __/__/__ TO SUN __/__/__

THE GOOD!

THE BAD...

THE NEUTRAL.

NEXT WEEK I'M LOOKING FORWARD TO:

MY BIGGEST CHALLENGE NEXT WEEK:

MESSAGE TO MYSELF FOR THIS TIME NEXT WEEK:

"Have go-to nutritional low effort food for days when you have low energy but still need to eat.

My go-to is tuna, rice cakes, protein yoghurt, cereal bars and pre-prepped salad or fruit. Obviously choose foods that you like and have some that store well."

– Kelly Harmer-Jones

Kelly is originally from North Wales but now lives in Berkshire. She is a development chef and mum.
She was diagnosed Autistic in her 30s and has since gone on a long journey of discovery to find out what the diagnosis means for her, and to practise being kinder to herself.

"Fitting in is overrated. Although in some ways it seems like it will feel safe, at the end of the day you need to be yourself - it's hard to spend all your time being someone else."

- CARLY X

ALL ABOUT TODAY __/__/__

THE BEST THING

THE WORST THING

THE WEATHER WAS:

MY FAVE MEAL WAS:

IF TODAY HAD A SOUNDTRACK THE SONG WOULD BE:

ALL ABOUT TODAY __/__/__

THE BEST THING

THE WORST THING

THE WEATHER WAS:

MY FAVE MEAL WAS:

IF TODAY HAD A SOUNDTRACK THE SONG WOULD BE:

ALL ABOUT TODAY __/__/__

THE BEST THING

THE WORST THING

THE WEATHER WAS:

MY FAVE MEAL WAS:

IF TODAY HAD A SOUNDTRACK THE SONG WOULD BE:

ALL ABOUT TODAY __/__/__

THE BEST THING

THE WORST THING

THE WEATHER WAS:

MY FAVE MEAL WAS:

IF TODAY HAD A SOUNDTRACK THE SONG WOULD BE:

ALL ABOUT TODAY __/__/__

THE BEST THING

THE WORST THING

THE WEATHER WAS:

MY FAVE MEAL WAS:

IF TODAY HAD A SOUNDTRACK THE SONG WOULD BE:

ALL ABOUT TODAY __/__/__

THE BEST THING

THE WORST THING

THE WEATHER WAS:

MY FAVE MEAL WAS:

IF TODAY HAD A SOUNDTRACK THE SONG WOULD BE:

ALL ABOUT TODAY __/__/__

THE BEST THING

THE WORST THING

THE WEATHER WAS:

MY FAVE MEAL WAS:

IF TODAY HAD A SOUNDTRACK THE SONG WOULD BE:

"You aren't the same as everyone else, and that's ok. It's great even! Take time and learn to love what it is that makes you special."

– CARLY X

ALL ABOUT THIS WEEK

MON __/__/__ TO SUN __/__/__

THE GOOD!

THE BAD...

THE NEUTRAL.

NEXT WEEK I'M LOOKING FORWARD TO:

MY BIGGEST CHALLENGE NEXT WEEK:

MESSAGE TO MYSELF FOR THIS TIME NEXT WEEK:

Well done for taking the time to complete this journal. I hope you've found it useful! What things do you feel you've learnt about yourself? You might like to take a few minutes to reflect on some of what you've written. Are there any things you always like (or always don't!)?

"

"

ADVICE

POINTS FOR PARENTS, CARERS AND SUPPORT TO CONSIDER

There is no rule around how often the young person should share the journal contents. This is a discussion to be had and something to be agreed upon between you.

For some, it may be that the journal is shared once it is completed. For example, it could be used to help the young person consider and then share their everyday life differences in a diagnostic appointment that will happen in a few months' time.

For those who are struggling with an eating disorder, depression or bullying, sharing each day may be more helpful.

Maybe if there is a lot of school or university anxiety, the journal could be shared once a week at a support appointment with a trusted teacher or non-medical assistant?

These agreements can also change if one week or month is particularly difficult or if a large life event occurs, but the agreement must be mutual, respectfully agreed upon and the young person should be given the opportunity to talk through why sharing might happen more or less often.

The journal may prove helpful to prompt a conversation. This should be led by the young person themselves and their words shouldn't be read without consent. The young person is showing great bravery and vulnerability in sharing their daily life and, as tempting as it might be for a caring and worried adult to want to help, the trust of the young person must be respected at all times. So no peeking unless allowed to peek! (Trust me, your young person will figure it out - we are smart as well as Autistic.)

WHAT SHOULD I BE LOOKING OUT FOR? ARE THERE ANY "RED FLAGS"?

There are many standard warning signs when it comes to safeguarding, including looking out for sudden new friendships, gifts from new people, recent arguments, etc.

As the parent or carer, it is less about spotting isolated incidents. (After all, Autistic young people are just like any other young people. We will make and lose new friends, we will be given token gifts from other who care about us, we will have arguments with others and fall out with friends and those we have relationships with, and more about looking for patterns.)

What are the triggers for your young person expressing unhappiness? Do the same issues appear frequently when they are writing about the worst part of their week? Don't forget to look through the "best" parts as well (that's where any unexpected gifts may appear!).

Each time you speak to your young person about their journal, try to explore any issues in a non-judgemental way. Ask open questions about what you've read or been told.

If your gut tells you that more safeguarding intervention is needed, don't ignore it. There are levels of support out there for any situation you are facing.

If the issue seems less serious/not urgent, your local Autism charity can help or will be able to signpost you to more advice.

If you think your young person might benefit from more targeted advice, they can contact support lines. Many of these now have text, email or online chat functions which can be particularly helpful for Autistic users. Numbers and organizations will differ from country to country, so it will be a case of searching online for the best method to use.

In a very serious situation, you can call the police non-emergency number for support.

In a urgent situation though, **ALWAYS** call the emergency services. This is one time to trust your instinct and not take any chances.

NOTES

by the same author

SAFEGUARDING AUTISTIC GIRLS
Strategies for Professionals
Carly Jones
Foreword by Luke Beardon
ISBN 978 1 78775 759 2
eISBN 978 1 78775 760 8

of related interest

THE AUTISM-FRIENDLY COOKBOOK
Lydia Wilkins
Illustrated by Emily of @21andsensory
ISBN 978 1 83997 082 5
eISBN 978 1 83997 083 2

KNOW YOUR SPECTRUM!
An Autism Creative Writing Workbook for Teens
Finn Monahan
ISBN 978 1 78592 435 4

THE AUTISTIC TEEN'S AVOIDANT EATING WORKBOOK
Elizabeth Shea
Illustrated by Tim Stringer
ISBN 978 1 78775 859 9
eISBN 978 1 78775 860 5